Outwitting
the Devil
ACTION GUIDE

Outwitting *the* Devil

◆

Napoleon Hill

AN OFFICIAL PUBLICATION OF
THE NAPOLEON HILL FOUNDATION

Published and distributed by:
SOUND WISDOM
P.O. Box 310
Shippensburg, PA 17257-0310
717-530-2122

info@soundwisdom.com
www.soundwisdom.com

While efforts have been made to verify information contained in this publication, neither the author nor the publisher assumes any responsibility for errors, inaccuracies, or omissions. While this publication is chock-full of useful, practical information; it is not intended to be legal or accounting advice. All readers are advised to seek competent lawyers and accountants to follow laws and regulations that may apply to specific situations. The reader of this publication assumes responsibility for the use of the information. The author and publisher assume no responsibility or liability whatsoever on the behalf of the reader of this publication.

The scanning, uploading and distribution of this publication via the Internet or via any other means without the permission of the publisher is illegal and punishable by law. Please purchase only authorized editions and do not participate in or encourage piracy of copyrightable materials.

Cover/jacket design by Eileen Rockwell
Interior design by Terry Clifton
Curated by Jennifer Janechek

ISBN 13 TP: 978-1-64095-189-1
ISBN 13 eBook: 978-1-64095-190-7

For Worldwide Distribution, Printed in China
1 2 3 4 5 6 7 8 / 25 24 23 22 21

A NOTE ON THE TEXT

THIS BOOK CONTAINS a summary of the original, unedited *Outwitting the Devil*, written by Napoleon Hill in 1938 and reprinted by Sound Wisdom in conjunction with the Napoleon Hill Foundation. A "combination of fact, fiction, and allegory," *Outwitting the Devil* details Hill's interview with the Devil, from whom Hill wrings a startling confession about the means the Devil uses to drag humans into failure through the habit of drifting. The Devil also discloses a formula that humans may use to break his control at their will.

Whether the Devil with whom Hill spoke was real or imaginary matters little to the profound truths detailed in this book—principles that, when studied individually and in the context of a book club or mastermind group and then applied through the action items offered in this book, will lead you on the path to self-determination and the peace of mind that true success brings.

Rather than taking you chapter by chapter through *Outwitting the Devil*, this book is organized into 20 core concepts to provide you with the most thorough understanding of the complex success theory developed in the original manuscript. Prepare your mind for the fact that many of the concepts challenge conventional wisdom. Hill does not ask you to believe everything proposed by the Devil—he himself did not. But by openly and thoughtfully considering the ideas, you will develop the strength of mind necessary to transform your greatest desires into reality.

> "Spiritual and economic freedom, the two highest aims of which human beings are capable, are available only through the proper use of the mind."

CONTENTS

CHAPTER 1

♦

ENERGY

Life consists of great swarms of energy, or entities,
each as intelligent as human beings believe themselves
to be. These units of life group themselves together
like hives of bees, and remain together until
they disintegrate, through lack of harmony.

HAVE YOU EVER FELT like there were warring impulses at work within your mind? Or have you ever been moving full-steam toward your goals, only to suddenly and inexplicably feel compelled to switch directions and veer off-course?

Such sensations occur because we have within ourselves both positive and negative forces vying for dominance. These opposing forces exist within units of energy—like positive and negative charges in an atom— that band together and exert influence over our thoughts and actions.

Because these forces determine our experience, it is crucial that we understand how they function and how we can manage and develop them to our advantage.

> "Your own thoughts and desires serve as the magnet which attracts units of life, from the great ocean of life. Only the friendly units which harmonize with the nature of your desires are attracted."

All living entities—humans, animals, and plants—are made up of units of energy. Each unit of energy contains an equal amount of intelligence. The difference between life forms results from the relative number of intelligence units housed within them. These units of energy control both our mental and physical functioning. Although no single unit of intelligence specializes in a particular activity, they group together and adopt a specific role in the body's operation. All of our senses—including the sixth sense, or the creative imagination—are controlled and operated by a different group of intelligence units. As such, the way we perceive and process stimuli in our environment depends on the coordination and activity of our intelligence units, which is why it is imperative to ensure they are working together harmoniously toward productive ends.

But how can we control forces whose existence we cannot even prove?

Although we cannot see these forces, we can feel them at work. As the questions that open this chapter suggest, we sense when there is disharmony or dysregulation in our psychological or bodily system. Similarly, we recognize when our thoughts and actions are aligning to produce positive momentum. As forms of energy, groups of intelligence units tend toward entropy, or disorganization. This disorganization results primarily from their constituent forces—the positive and negative charges—contending for expression. Although both positive and negative forces will always exist in equal proportion within an individual intelligence unit, one expression can assume dominance over the other. When the negative portion of an intelligence unit achieves primacy in expression, other units of life harmonize with it and quickly follow suit, leaving us prone to a state of aimlessness known as drifting (the subject of chapter 4). On the other hand, when the negative portion goes dormant, we are empowered to act with definiteness and power.

Internal disorganization results not only because intelligence units contain both negative and positive charges, but also because they have different natures. As the First Law of Thermodynamics tells us, energy can neither be created nor destroyed; therefore, our units of life are not original to us—they derive from units on the spiritual plane of existence. We are born with a conglomerate of intelligence units and add to our collection as we journey through life—as our thoughts attract other intelligence units from the spiritual plane that harmonize with our own. Our dominating thoughts become magnetized when they are colored by strong emotion, whether positive or negative, and attract other groups of intelligence units through a process similar to resonance. These units have differences of opinion, just as do human beings, and often fight among themselves. Their disagreements pull us in different directions, creating internal strife that leads to indecisiveness.

> ### *What do you think about...eternal life?*
> According to the Devil, heaven and hell do not exist, but there is a spiritual plane of existence that coexists with the physical. When we die, our units of life transfer to the spiritual realm, where we retain our identity only if our state of mind is characterized by peace and harmony. If our mental state is marked by fear or violence, our units of life become disorganized and disperse after death.

One of the key insights shared by the Devil is just how crucial inner harmony is, not only to our mental and physical health, but also to our success. As humans, we can use the power of our thoughts to foster this state of harmony by heightening the expression of, as well as enlarging, our storehouse of positive energy. By stimulating our thoughts and desires with positive emotions such as faith, we can attract more positive energy—intelligence units in which the positive charge is dominant in expression—from our surroundings. This principle works in reverse as well: if we emotionalize our thoughts with negative feelings like greed, despair, and fear, we will attract negative energy, and our thought habits will suffer accordingly. It is therefore crucial that we center our thoughts on the certainty of attaining what we most desire in life, whether that be professional success, peace of mind, strong relationships, a legacy of service, or another such worthy goal. The more positive energy we express and attract, the more we are empowered to act with definiteness and power.

Steps to Self-Determination

How would you characterize your current internal state? Would you describe it as organized and well-regulated or, alternately, as uncoordinated and inharmonious? How might insights from this chapter enable you to regain control over your energy so that you are well-positioned for success?

CHAPTER 2

◆

THE SIXTH SENSE

*Somewhere in the cell structure of the brain
is located an organ which receives vibrations
of thought ordinarily called "hunches."*

ONCE WE LEARN TO protect and cultivate our energy, we can take
advantage of a sixth sense—the creative imagination. Through this
mode of perception, we can access thought impulses from the universal storehouse of energy, or what might be termed Infinite Intelligence.
Thought impulses deriving from the sixth sense provide the only means
of creating new knowledge; the other mode of knowledge production,
alternately termed the synthetic imagination or the reasoning faculty,
functions by combining existing information in different ways to generate productive insight.

You might have already encountered the sixth sense unknowingly...

Have you ever experienced a "hunch," a flash of inspiration, that seemed to derive from a supernatural source—one that, when followed, proved to be crucial to avoiding disaster or seizing a rare opportunity?

Chances are, this sensation was the creative imagination at work, granting you access to original insight not available by any other means. When in operation, the sixth sense generally produces a calming sensation, followed by the feeling of a thought abruptly and forcefully bursting into one's mind. Although spoken by an internal voice, the thought typically seems like it derives from an outside source, so powerful and certain is the knowledge communicated. While the impulse emerges from external intelligence, it is not a supernatural phenomenon. As with everything in the universe, the sixth sense is governed by natural law, which is absolute and unyielding in its principles.

> ### What do you think about...miracles?
> Although incredible things may happen in our lives, they are not the result of so-called "miracles." Everything that happens in the world can be explained by inviolable natural laws. That doesn't mean that prayers aren't answered; it simply means that they are answered only through natural forces. Through prayer, we are able to receive plans from Infinite Intelligence, but we are ultimately responsible for implementing them.

When our mind is under the influence of some form of extraordinary stimulation—as when we are under extreme pressure, facing a difficult challenge, or experiencing intense emotion—it becomes more receptive to the thought impulses being broadcast by other humans' minds and the collective intelligence in the spiritual plane. The following are mental stimulants that can be used to activate the sixth sense by increasing the rate of vibration of our thought impulses:

- Sexual desire
- Love
- Burning desire for fame, power, or wealth
- Music
- Friendship
- Mastermind alliance
- Adversity
- Positive affirmations

Fear sometimes serves as a mental stimulant, but more often than not it is counterproductive, because it can inhibit the mind's receptivity to external communications.

As the quotation that opens this chapter indicates, somewhere in the brain is an organ—a group of intelligence units—responsible for receiving and processing these thought impulses, translating them into language. The translation is not always perfect, however, as human language is inadequate compared to the language of thought. But knowledge produced by the creative imagination is still far superior to that produced by human insight alone.

Indeed, there is great power in cultivating an awareness of when and how the sixth sense is at work. When we receive these communications as accurate knowledge rather than dismissing them as "instinct" or "superstition," we are better prepared to translate them into definite plans and take action accordingly. For who would dismiss the commands of the sixth sense, whose urgency and deliberateness promise to help humans actualize their chief desires?

Those who sharpen their sixth sense can even use it to communicate with groups of intelligence units on the spiritual plane. For instance, humans might use it to assemble a panel of Invisible Counselors, mentors—both living and dead—who help us develop the character qualities we most desire. The sixth sense is the means by which the Devil's confession was extracted.

Steps to Self-Determination

Activate the sixth sense by directing sustained and emotionalized thought toward the certainty of your ultimate success in attaining what you most desire in life. Write three affirmations below that will boost your confidence in your ability to fulfill your definite major purpose. Recite these affirmations morning and night, using one of the positive mental stimulants listed in this chapter to heighten the frequency of your thought impulses.

CHAPTER 3

THE LANGUAGE OF THOUGHT

There is no language on this plane, save the language of thought. All thought is universally understood.

THOUGHTS ARE THINGS. Although they do not take up space, they are a form of energy—electric impulses—that can be transmitted, attracted, and stored. Our brains, functioning like a receiving station, collect these thought impulses and organize them into definite thought forms. In order to succeed, we must protect our minds from destructive energy and harness the power of constructive thoughts to act on our definite major purpose. Doing so requires us to filter and decipher thought impulses properly and use them to construct well-structured thought forms.

> ### *What do you think about...telepathy?*
> Those on the spiritual plane are able to fully understand each other's communications without the limitations of spoken or written language. On the physical plane, the sixth sense allows humans to communicate in thought impulses as well as to appropriate thought impulses from Infinite Intelligence and spiritual entities.

Autosuggestion is the principle by which our most intense and recurring thoughts find outlet in actions that translate them into their material counterpart. When we are not intentional about filtering thought impulses received by our mind, we risk developing negative thought habits that, through autosuggestion, generate destructive and disordered plans that derail our success journey. As the Devil explains, Nature abhors a vacuum, and in the absence of definite thoughts of a positive nature, the mind fills with aimless, negative thoughts. These negative thoughts organize themselves into destructive thought habits and, if left untreated, are taken over by hypnotic rhythm, which renders them permanent. Idle minds—more so than idle hands—are the Devil's workshop.

The Devil also uses apathetic minds to plant the seeds of his own ideas, causing those individuals to become agents of his propaganda. Thoughts of fear, discouragement, hopelessness, and destructiveness grant the Devil power over our mind. Accurate thinking is the key to safeguarding our mind from the Devil's influence. It is characterized by the following qualities:

- Freedom from dogma, bias, or the need for approval from others

- The emotions of faith, courage, hope, and definiteness of purpose

Openness, positivity, and resolve generate accurate thought, which seeks outlet in concrete, practical plans. Accurate thoughts enlist the law of hypnotic rhythm to support our success by enabling us to build structures of thought, relationships, and plans that aid the translation of our desire into reality.

> "The person who thinks in terms of power, success, and opulence, sets up a rhythm which attracts these desirable possessions. The person who thinks in terms of misery, failure, defeat, discouragement, and poverty attracts these undesirable influences. This explains why both success and failure are the result of habit. Habit establishes one's rhythm of thought, and that rhythm attracts the object of one's dominating thoughts."

From a seed to a spiral...

Have you ever been swept along a path of toxic thinking and felt unable to extricate yourself from the downward spiral—a cycle that began with only the tiniest seed of a negative thought or passive desire? Alternatively, have you experienced the incredible momentum that results from intentional, constructive thought habits—patterns that have their root in a single positive thought impulse? If so, then you have witnessed the power of autosuggestion, which works together with hypnotic rhythm to the benefit or detriment of the individual, depending on the nature of our thoughts.

Except in very rare circumstances, we have control over our thoughts. Do not leave your mind open to the influence of the destructive forces of the world, as they will thwart your pursuit of your definite major purpose. Instead, become fluent in the language of thought by learning to focus and organize the impulses in your brain. This process involves the following steps:

1. Intentionally fix your mind on your most burning desires. It can be helpful to contextualize your desires by situating them within a motive structure. The nine most common constructive motives for inspiring physical action are as follows:

    ▸ The desire for sex expression and love

    ▸ The desire for physical food

    ▸ The desire for spiritual, mental, and physical self-expression

    ▸ The desire for perpetuation of life after death

    ▸ The desire for power over others

    ▸ The desire for material wealth

    ▸ The desire for knowledge

    ▸ The desire to imitate others

    ▸ The desire to excel over others

2. Emotionalize these desires with one or more of the following the positive emotions:

    ▶ Faith

    ▶ Love

    ▶ Sex

    ▶ Enthusiasm

    ▶ Romance

    ▶ Hope

3. Use repetition to activate autosuggestion and enable hypnotic rhythm to cement your thought habits into actions.

Steps to Self-Determination

Cultivate an awareness of your mind's susceptibility to the habit of drifting by recording instances when you notice your thoughts becoming negative, passive, and/or disorganized. Can you identify any patterns? For example, is there a particular time of day, activity, or feeling that seems to correlate with destructive thoughts? Based on your observations, how can you modify your thoughts and behaviors to better protect yourself from the Devil's influence?

CHAPTER 4

◆

DRIFTING

No one ever drifts into anything but failure!

DRIFTING IS THE CONDITION by which passive, negative, and disorganized thinking translates into habits of aimlessness and procrastination that drive an individual toward failure. It is the primary cause of an individual's loss of freedom and success, for peace of mind is found in freedom of thought and purposeful service to others. As the last chapter explains, passive thinking—leaving your mind open to outside influences and allowing disorganized, unfiltered thoughts to circulate through it—grants the Devil power over your thoughts, emotions, and behaviors.

Drifters do little to no thinking for themselves. They allow themselves to be influenced, and ultimately controlled, by external thoughts and occurrences. Drifting causes failure for three main reasons:

- It allows the Devil to mold an individual in whatever way he chooses.

- It destroys personal initiative.

- It prevents the Devil's opposition—what some call "God"—from intervening.

> "A life that is lived with fullness of peace of mind, contentment and happiness always divests itself of everything it does not want! Anyone who submits to annoyance by things he does not want is not definite. He is a drifter!"

How can you identify a drifter when you encounter one? How can you determine whether you suffer from drifting? The Devil provides the following signs that you're in the presence of a drifter:

- A drifter lacks a definite major purpose in life.

- A drifter lacks self-confidence.

- A drifter will not accomplish anything requiring thought and effort, nor will he find the enthusiasm or initiative to undertake any project that he is not forced into.

- A drifter will take the easiest route to complete a task.

- A drifter is a spendthrift who often abuses credit much to his detriment.

- A drifter often suffers from hypochondria and seeks spiritual intervention for even the slightest physical distress.

- A drifter lacks imagination.

- A drifter is emotionally volatile and often in ill humor.

- A drifter lacks charisma and rarely attracts other individuals with his personality.

- A drifter has opinions on everything but accurate knowledge of nothing.

- A drifter might be a jack-of-all-trades but excel at nothing.

- A drifter is not inclined to cooperate with those around him, even those on whom he depends for food and shelter.

- A drifter never learns from failure and will make the same mistake repeatedly.

- A drifter is narrow-minded and intolerant of differences in opinion.

- A drifter demands the best from others but gives little or nothing in return.

- A drifter begins many projects but will rarely complete something.

- A drifter is a vocal critic of the government but cannot provide definite opinions on how to improve it.

- A drifter is compulsively indecisive and, when forced to make a decision, will try to reverse it at the first chance.

- A drifter overeats and exercises little.

- A drifter drinks only on someone else's tab and gambles only on credit.

- A drifter criticizes others who are succeeding in their calling.

- A drifter will tell a lie rather than admit ignorance.

- A drifter will gossip about people behind their backs and flatter the same individuals to their faces.

> "The drifter will work harder to get out of thinking than most others work in earning a good living."

Because of their laziness, complacency, and ignorance, drifters are excellent pawns for the Devil, who uses them to spread unrest, fantasy, and fear within society.

Only 2 percent of the world's population attain their definite major purpose in life.

Non-drifters, the 2 percent of the world who achieve true and lasting success, possess the following qualities:

- A non-drifter is always engaged in definite action backed by a definite, well-organized plan.
- A non-drifter's sense of purpose is evident in the tone of his voice, the firmness of his step, the gleam in his eyes, and the quickness of his decisions.
- A non-drifter provides direct answers to all questions.
- A non-drifter showers favors on others but rarely accepts them in return.
- A non-drifter can always be found at the frontlines of a game or battle.
- A non-drifter will admit when he does not know an answer.
- A non-drifter remembers and openly admits all his failings.
- A non-drifter never blames others for mistakes, even if it is his fault.

- A non-drifter is a "go-giver": he is characterized by high achievement that trickles down to others.
- A non-drifter is a great source of inspiration to others.

Whereas drifters do not think for themselves, non-drifters exercise the right to independent thought in all areas of life. They view it as a freedom to celebrate and protect above all else. Drifters, on the other hand, shirk responsibility and look for success in handouts.

> "The non-drifter takes from Life whatever he wants, but he takes it on his terms! The drifter takes whatever he can get, but he takes what he gets on [the Devil's] terms."

How does the Devil lock humans into the habit of drifting?

The following are the Devil's favorite tools for luring humans into the habit of drifting:

- Procrastination/indecision
- Fear
- Flattery
- Propaganda
- Failure

These tools can be leveraged in different types of environments, including:

- **Education:** The Devil induces children to go through school without any clear direction. This foundation of indirection leads to indirection in everything.

- **Health:** The Devil encourages people to eat too much food and the wrong types of foods, causing indigestion and preventing accurate thinking.

- **Marriage:** The Devil entices people to get married without any plan for how a harmonious relationship will be possible. Then, he causes married people to fight over money issues, differences in parenting styles, their friendships outside of marriage, and their social activities.

- **Occupation:** The Devil encourages people to drift from school into the first available job they can find, with little forethought about their career possibilities or future happiness.

- **Savings:** The Devil inspires people to spend without reserve and save very little, if at all, so that he can control them entirely through the fear of poverty.

- **Environment:** The Devil lures people into inharmonious, toxic environments in their home, their workplace, and their relationships with friends and family, and then he encourages people to remain there.

- **Dominating thoughts:** The Devil fills idle minds with negative thoughts, which lead to destructive behaviors, which in turn lead to controversies and fears. These negative thoughts derive primarily from religious authorities, news media, and popular entertainment (television, film, music, and art).

Luckily, the Devil provides a formula against drifting.

Because drifting is a habit, it can be avoided altogether and, if developed, overcome...as long as the habit is broken before hypnotic rhythm takes hold of it. The methods the Devil describes to conquer the habit of drifting are available to every individual of sound body and mind:

- Do your own thinking on all occasions.

- Decide definitively what you want from life, then create a plan for attaining it, and be willing to sacrifice everything else, if necessary, rather than accept permanent defeat.

- Analyze all temporary defeat and extract from it the seed of an equivalent advantage.

- Be willing to render useful service equal in value to the material things you demand of life—and do it before you expect anything in return.

- Activate your sixth sense and tune into the communications of Infinite Intelligence.

- Invest your most valuable asset and the only one you own outright—time—in worthy pursuits, budgeting it so that none is wasted.

- Recognize that fear is filler, used by the Devil to occupy the unused portions of your mind so that he can grow destructive thought habits, and that you can avoid and cure this state of mind by filling the space it occupies with faith in your ability to make Life provide you with whatever you demand of it.

- Pray without begging. Demand what you want of Life and insist upon getting exactly that, with no substitutes.

- Refuse to accept from Life anything you do not want! If something you don't want is forced upon you, then refuse to accept it and your mind will make way for the thing you do want.

- Be careful what your thoughts dwell upon, as your dominating thoughts attract their physical counterpart through the shortest and most convenient route.

Of course, service matters too, as the Devil says elsewhere that the best cure for drifting is rendering useful service to as many people as possible.

> "Be definite in everything you do and never leave unfinished thoughts in the mind. Form the habit of reaching definite decisions on all subjects!"

Steps to Self-Determination

Revisit the inventory of characteristics used to describe a drifter. Which of these qualities do you currently possess? Make a plan below for eliminating them and replacing them with traits common to the non-drifter.

CHAPTER 5

HYPNOTIC RHYTHM

*Any impulse of thought the mind repeats over and
over through habit forms an organized rhythm.*

WE ALL KNOW THE power of habit: do anything enough, and it
becomes increasingly easy to continue the same behavior—and increasingly difficult to do it any other way. Habits are like grooves in the mind
carved out by repeated thoughts and actions. As we engage in the same
thought patterns, our brains default to the same experiences.

Not all thought habits are created equal: some strengthen willpower,
while others weaken it. Once a negative habit is established, others are
much more likely to take root in the mind. As the Devil explains, "Habits
come in pairs, triplets, and quadruplets. Any habit which weakens one's
willpower invites quadruplets. Any habit which weakens one's willpower
invites a flock of its relatives to move in and take possession of the mind."

> ### *What do you think about...habits?*
> Regardless of how seemingly constructive a habit is, we should never run on autopilot to the extent that we lose freedom of thought, for the inactive mind is subject to the Devil's machinations. All habits should be directed toward a purposeful end, and they should be cultivated and maintained with intentionality.

Both "good" and "bad" habits are subject to control by hypnotic rhythm, a universal law through which Nature maintains a perfect balance by fixing permanently, through rhythm, the repeated thoughts and behaviors of humans. The Devil entraps people through hypnotic rhythm first by gaining access to their mind through traits that are inborn to humans, such as:

- Fear
- Superstition
- Avarice
- Greed
- Lust
- Revenge
- Anger
- Vanity
- Laziness

Then the Devil manipulates these natural tendencies to establish habits that weaken an individual's willpower. One by one, mental habits are cultivated that lead to habits of behavior, until the Devil seizes complete control of one's mind.

What do you think about...the Devil?

Do not make the mistake of envisioning a caricatured Devil: there is no red demon with a spiky tail and pitchfork prodding your mind to win you over to the dark side; the Devil is merely representative of the negative forces that oppose the good ones in the universe.

The law of hypnotic rhythm is the controlling force behind all success principles.

No success principle can be implemented effectively without understanding and coordinating with the law of hypnotic rhythm. The law of gravity and all other natural laws that maintain a balance of forces are merely expressions of the law of hypnotic rhythm. The Devil explains that there is "a universal form of energy with which nature keeps a perfect balance between all matter and energy." Nature divides this universal building material into different wavelengths through the formation of habits. As habits become fixed in the mind, they harmonize to form a structured pattern—a pattern that takes on its own nature when guided by the larger force of hypnotic rhythm.

"If the same thought is held in the mind, or left there by neglect, for a certain length of time, nature takes it over, through the rhythm of habit, and makes it permanent."

Undesirable habits can be broken, but they must be conquered before they reach the proportions of rhythm. Once habit, through repetition, attains the level of rhythm, the habit cannot be broken because Nature assumes control and renders it permanent. Think of a whirlpool: it will ensnare an object and carry it round and round indefinitely. Human thought occurs via wavelengths of energy that can be likened to the water in a river. A thought is like an object in that river: it will float along unobstructed until it is held in the mind for too long, whether intentionally or through neglect, whereby Nature takes over and fixes its path as permanent, with no means of escape. The location of the whirlpool differs for each individual, but once you encounter it, it becomes near impossible to throw off the habit of drifting and reclaim the right to use your own mind.

How can you break the habit of drifting before hypnotic rhythm renders it permanent?

Useless or destructive habits, both of which are harmful in their own way, can be broken through the following eight means:

- A burning desire to break the habit
- Definiteness of purpose
- Self-discipline

- The ability to learn from adversity
- Environment
- Time
- Harmony
- Caution

The first principle—the strong desire to break the habit before it solidifies into a permanent rhythm—counters the indifference that first fostered the habit of drifting. Apathy and a lack of ambition breed listlessness, which enables the Devil to gain a foothold in an individual's mind. The remaining seven concepts are the subjects of the next seven chapters.

Steps to Self-Determination

The Devil admits that "hypnotic rhythm is something to be studied, understood, and voluntarily applied to attain definite *desired* ends." How would you summarize the law of hypnotic rhythm in your own words? Are there any examples you could provide of its application?

_____

_____

_____

_____

_____

_____

_____

_____

_____

_____

_____

_____

_____

_____

_____

_____

_____

_____

What thought habits do you currently have that might be negatively worked upon by hypnotic rhythm? Make a plan for forming thought habits that will enable you to harness the power of hypnotic rhythm to your advantage.

CHAPTER 6

◆

Definiteness of Purpose

*All habits, save that of definiteness,
may lead to the habit of drifting!*

THE FIRST PRINCIPLE FOR breaking the habit of drifting before hypnotic rhythm fixes it as permanent is definiteness of purpose. When we possess the quality of definiteness, we have a singular focus, a thorough understanding of our motivations and aims, a firmness in our resolve, and an unwillingness to accept defeat as final. Definiteness is what transforms intentions into actions.

The road to hell is paved with good intentions.

If a good intention does not attain the quality of definiteness, it can lead to drifting, which, through the workings of hypnotic rhythm, does indeed lead to psychological and physical hell. Intentions trick us into thinking we are doing well because we mean well. However, thought without the structure of habit quickly gives rise to the aimlessness characterized by drifting. We are thus tasked with transforming our intentions into a definite purpose backed by definite plans.

> ### What do you think about...love as a threat to definiteness?
> The Devil acknowledges that "every principle of good carries with it the seed of an equivalent danger." The love of anything, except definiteness, can be dangerous, as love can suppress willpower and accurate thinking. For this reason, the Devil lists love and fear as his two most effective weapons for seducing people into the habit of drifting. Individuals who are overcome by either love or fear cannot take full advantage of the principle of definiteness, by which they can prevent the law of hypnotic rhythm from rendering their destructive habits permanent.

If you do not want life's leftovers—if you want to rise above the 98 percent of individuals who lack a definite aim in life—then you need to identify your definite major purpose, the one thing you desire above all else in life. This might be monetary in nature, or it might have to do with amassing power, or it might pertain to the quality of your relationships—it is up to you to decide how you will define success.

> "The person who does not know precisely what he wants of Life must accept whatever Life has left over after those who use definiteness as a policy get through choosing."

A definite major purpose is more than a thought impulse; it is a state of mind through which a desire is nurtured into an all-encompassing drive to achieve a specific aim, backed by faith in the certainty of one's success in attaining it. A definite major purpose has three characteristics:

- It is definite; it has specificity.
- It is dominating; it takes primacy over all other thoughts.
- It is supported by faith, or the certainty that you will achieve it.

Everything we think and do should be in complete alignment with this definite major purpose, and any obstacles that come in the way of it should be approached as opportunities to increase our effort and innovate, rather than an excuse to give up on our dreams.

Definiteness in the small things leads to definiteness in the big things.

Definiteness is like a muscle that can be strengthened through regular exercise. As you practice definiteness in the mundane aspects of your life, you will be better equipped to apply definiteness to your chief aim in life. For example, making a definite decision about the time you'll wake up in the morning—setting an alarm and arising with definiteness, at its first call—creates momentum that fuels your definiteness throughout the rest of the day.

Be aware that the Devil will try to counter your efforts by tempting you with thought habits in which you find it pleasurable to indulge. If, for instance, you have a penchant for travel, you'll be tricked into daydreaming about a vacation rather than taking the definite steps you need to turn your vision into reality.

In order to translate our primary desire into its material counterpart, we can make use of the formula for definiteness found below.

Formula for Definiteness of Purpose

1. Establish in your mind the exact object you desire (e.g., a specific sum of money, a specific position, a specific relationship, etc.).
2. Determine specifically what you are willing to give in exchange for attaining your definite aim.
3. Set a firm deadline for acquiring your definite aim.
4. Create, and immediately begin implementing, a definite plan for achieving your definite aim. Do not rely on logic or reason alone; revisit the chapter on the sixth sense for help using the creative imagination to generate practical plans.
5. Condense your responses to the above four steps and write them in a clear, concise statement.
6. Read this statement aloud to yourself twice daily—once just before bed and once soon after

> waking up. As you recite your definite major purpose, see, feel, and believe yourself to be already in possession of what you desire.

Another way of expressing this formula is the statement that "one's dominating desires can be crystallized into their physical equivalents through definiteness of purpose backed by definiteness of plans, with the aid of nature's law of hypnotic rhythm and Time!" If you can remember and live out this recipe for definiteness, you can be victorious in life.

Definiteness inspires innovation, cultivates influence, and attracts riches.

Definiteness of purpose is what separates truly successful individuals from those who succumb to the negative workings of hypnotic rhythm. It is what catapulted Henry Ford, Franklin D. Roosevelt, and Thomas Edison to success, and it is what brought Hitler and Al Capone to power (and infamy). Those who lack definiteness are no match for individuals who possess this quality. What will be your weapon against drifting and your key to success?

> "Any human being who can be definite in his aims and plans can make Life hand over whatever is wanted!"

Steps to Self-Determination

Write a list below of obstacles to definiteness in your life. Consider good intentions, natural inclinations, thought habits, environmental influences, and other gateways to drifting. Identify three constructive thought habits that will help you maintain definiteness when these temptations arise.

CHAPTER 7

◆

SELF-DISCIPLINE

The person who is not master of himself
can never be master of others.

IN ORDER TO THINK and act with definiteness of purpose, we must possess the quality of self-control, or self-discipline. Indeed, the most destructive form of indefiniteness is the lack of self-mastery. The five remaining safeguards against drifting (learning from adversity, environment, time, harmony, and caution) are all expressions of the principle of self-discipline. The Devil goes so far as to say that human beings should emulate him because he never loses self-control. Then again, neither does his opposition, as both are restricted by the functioning of natural law. Only humans have the privilege of independence of thought, whereby they can act against natural law. Of course, their violation can only ever be temporary. The law of compensation, one manifestation of hypnotic rhythm, ensures that individuals eventually reap what they sow in equal measure.

There are four primary appetites that everyone must master in order to develop enough self-discipline to avoid the snare of drifting:

- The desire for food
- The desire for expression of sex
- The desire to express loosely organized opinions
- The desire to indulge in spiritual orgies through some form of religious ceremony

Because they are natural appetites, they cannot be avoided entirely, but this fact offers us the opportunity to develop willpower and resolve, to cultivate an appreciation for moderation and balance, and to improve our ability to channel our natural desires toward productive ends.

What do you think about...the law of compensation?

In his essay "Compensation," Ralph Waldo Emerson describes how every human being is rewarded or punished in life according to the nature of their actions. The punishment might not seem directly related to the wrong—it might be delayed, or it might adopt a different expression (such as fear rather than apparent failure)—but it is in some way tied to the infraction. Hypnotic rhythm ensures that all forces are balanced in a harmonious manner. The same principle applies to constructive thoughts and actions: render useful service to others and foster harmonious relations, and the universe will reward you in an equivalent, but not necessarily identical, manner.

Your stomach and your brain are linked.

Eating too much food, especially the wrong kinds of food, affects the quality of your thoughts. Overindulgence in rich, unhealthy food slows digestion, physical movement, and cognition, causing us to become irritable and anxious and to lose the ability to focus or think critically. To master the desire for food, we must attend to the quantity and quality of the food we consume and ensure that our diet has enough fiber to maintain an efficient internal system. More on how to control this natural appetite can be found in chapter 11.

Sex is a productive desire...when channeled appropriately.

Overindulgence in sex drains our creative and physical energy, effectively destroying our charisma, diminishing enthusiasm, and provoking negativity. Because it subdues ambition and personal initiative, it results in listlessness. However, the complete stifling of the emotion of sex causes it to break out into other, less desirable forms. To develop self-control in this area, convert the sex emotion into the driving force behind your professional pursuits. If you channel it properly, you will develop the magnetic force characteristic of a pleasing personality, vigor in tone and demeanor, momentum in your success journey, improved physical and mental health, enhanced creativity, more efficient and definite decision-making, ease of overcoming obstacles, immunity to the lures of laziness and procrastination, and more.

People who talk too much usually think too little.

The desire to express loosely organized opinions is inherent within all of us. We speak too much too soon because we want to feed our vanity and ego; we desire attention. However, sharing our thoughts too freely tends to have the opposite effect: it alienates your audience and destroys self-respect. This compulsion is the reason we have so much misinformation in the world: it influences people to guess instead of searching for the facts when they form opinions, create ideas, or organize plans. It causes scattered thinking and actions, to the extent that an individual will start many projects but rarely complete one. When we overshare, we invite others to profit from or interfere with our own ideas. However, there is great power in thoughtfully considered, well-researched ideas that are communicated with emotion, coherence, and definiteness. Seek to listen and learn primarily and to share your thoughts only when the situation calls for concise, measured speech.

Religious emotion makes people prone to unsound thinking.

The Devil does not take issue with religious expression because it opposes his aims; in fact, as will be covered in chapter 15, most religious expression strengthens his grip over the world. Innate to humans is a desire to engage in religious ceremonies that transport them into a state of spiritual and emotional rapture. Motivated primarily by fear of the Devil and the afterlife, these experiences break people's connection with Infinite Intelligence because they destroy reason, willpower, and the foundation of sound judgment and accurate thinking, thereby inviting the negative workings of hypnotic rhythm. The desire to indulge in spiritual orgies ultimately can lead to permanent loss of mental equilibrium. To strengthen your self-discipline in the domain of religious expression, realize that there is nothing for good or evil throughout all universes except the power of natural law.

Steps to Self-Determination

Describe below how you struggle to control one or more of the four natural appetites. Then, make a plan for mastering them using the principles outlined in this chapter.

_____

_____

_____

_____

_____

_____

_____

_____

_____

_____

_____

_____

_____

_____

_____

_____

_____

_____

_____

_____

_____

CHAPTER 8

---◆---

LEARNING FROM ADVERSITY

Failure is a man-made circumstance. It is never real
until it has been accepted by man as permanent.

CONTRARY TO WHAT WE tell ourselves, adversity is not the result of bad luck or ill fate. Even if we do not personally deserve a negative outcome, we might encounter trials because of our thoughts and behaviors as a family, community, nation, or even global society. The law of compensation applies to collective habits as much as it does to individual ones, ensuring that what we put into a system is equivalent to what emerges from it. Natural law, ever focused on maintaining and restoring harmony, guarantees that compounded negative thought habits and actions will result in adversity. With the assistance of time, hypnotic rhythm consolidates a series of circumstances into a discernable pattern—a groove of mental and behavioral habits—that eventually manifest as individual misfortune or, on a larger scale, economic depression and other mass afflictions.

Failure is never final.

Regardless of why we encounter misfortune, how we respond to it is the most important factor in determining our result. Failure is never final until it is viewed as such. However, the vast majority of individuals begin to drift as soon as they meet with opposition, and according to the Devil, "not one out of ten thousand will keep on trying after failing two or three times." Failure causes most people to drift because it diminishes morale, self-confidence, enthusiasm, imagination, and definiteness of purpose. As these qualities erode, we are more likely to accept temporary defeat as failure, rather than using it to fuel our success.

But failure does not have to dictate our outcomes—if we have the right mindset. As the Devil discloses, "Life gives to everyone the power of positive thought which is sufficient to master all circumstances of adversity and convert them into benefits." Mindset is entirely democratic: no matter your station in life, you can control your thoughts in a way that will mobilize you toward achieving your definite major purpose in life.

> "Every adversity brings with it the seed of an equivalent advantage."

In order to survive—and even thrive—in challenging times, we must remember two things:

- No matter how difficult a problem may seem, there is always a solution—if not one that will "fix" the issue, at least one that will offer a productive path forward.

- There is potential for great success within all temporary defeat—*if* it is approached as motivation to seek new plans and identify new opportunities.

Every great leader, entrepreneur, and innovator encounters difficulties and meets with temporary defeat before he or she "arrives." What distinguishes these individuals from the average person is that they possess a crucial quality called stickability: they persist through life's challenges and emerge victorious. Not only do they surmount failure, but they look within it to find the seeds of success. Consider the examples set by Thomas Edison and Henry Ford: neither of them gave up when they met with roadblocks in their path to innovation. Their success was in direct proportion to their ability to withstand temporary defeat. Most often, failure does not occur because of ineptitude but simply because an individual quits.

> "Success usually is but one short step beyond the point where one quits fighting."

Adversity offers an opportunity to reset for success.

While failure can induce or strengthen the habit of drifting, it can also break the grip of hypnotic rhythm because it offers the opportunity to completely reset the mind and start anew. Failure sometimes forces us to reach a level of crisis so intense that it enables us to clear our mind of any fear, break destructive habits, and make a new start in another direction, where we can create a new, more constructive rhythm. Take a moment to appreciate the following benefits of adversity:

- Adversity forces us to discover our weaknesses and to compensate for them.

- Adversity gives us a chance to test ourselves and learn how much willpower we have.

- Adversity forces us to learn many truths we might not otherwise discover.

- Adversity helps us appreciate the power of self-discipline to keep us out of the grip of hypnotic rhythm.

- Adversity enables us to discern the fault in our aims or plans to achieve those aims.

- Adversity cures us of vanity and egotism.

- Adversity inhibits selfishness and encourages collaboration and interdependence.

- Adversity pushes us toward meditation and introspection in order to find ways and means to definite ends, which often leads to discovery and use of the sixth sense.

- Adversity challenges us to recognize the need for intelligence from outside sources.

- Adversity breaks old thought habits and offers the opportunity to form new thought habits, thereby changing the operation of hypnotic rhythm from negative to positive ends.

The latter advantage is by far the greatest, for nothing else can break and redirect the force of hypnotic rhythm like adversity can. In order to translate adversity into opportunity, we should consult the resources available to us:

- The synthetic imagination, otherwise known as the reasoning faculty
- The creative imagination, otherwise known as the sixth sense
- Your mastermind group
- Your "other self"

The "other self" is the force that helps us break the grip of hypnotic rhythm when adversity and failure unsettle pre-existing patterns. It appears "at times of unusual emergency, when men are forced, through adversity and temporary defeat, to change their habits and think their way out of difficulty." When we hit "rock bottom"—when we think we are entirely out of options and have no earthly idea how we will get ourselves out of a difficult situation—it is then that we often hear the promptings of the other self, a faith entity that "knows no limitations, has no fears, and recognizes no such word as 'impossible.'" Unlike the fear entity, which prompts us to accept defeat, the other self provides us with the confidence we need to identify definite plans for recovering from failure.

The other self functions by joining with the sixth sense to generate new insight as to how to attain our definite major purpose. It communicates its inspiration through the medium of thoughts that arise with such force that they are easily distinguishable from our ordinary, self-generated ones. It overpowers the fear entity by weaning us from our inferiority complex, our feeling of not being good enough. Although the other self can dethrone the fear entity, the latter never dies; it simply goes dormant, awaiting the opportunity to regain dominance. Accordingly, we must tune into the faith entity and protect our minds from limiting, fear-based thoughts.

> "There is a great power to be discovered in your 'other self'! Search sincerely and you will find it."

Steps to Self-Determination

Reflecting on your life experience up to this point, what opportunities can you identify as having arisen out of difficulties and failures? Based on this insight, can you discern the seeds of success that might be hidden within current obstacles or challenges that you are facing?

CHAPTER 9

◆

ENVIRONMENT

All people absorb and take over, either
consciously or unconsciously, the thought habits
of those with whom they associate closely.

OUR ENVIRONMENT IS THE key to our success or our failure. Because our mind can never be idle, it is always absorbing external sensory input—for good or for bad. As such, we must attend to the physical and emotional forces acting upon us at any given time.

Each environment has its own definite, discernable rhythm, and the more we spend time in a particular environment, the more our thoughts align themselves with its rhythm, literally adjusting their tempo to reach the same rate of vibration. As hypnotic rhythm works upon our thoughts and our environments, the rhythm of both will become permanent with time.

> ### What do you think about...nature vs. nurture?
> It is often said that "we are the average of the five people with whom we spend the most time." The law of hypnotic rhythm provides physical justification for this: Nature causes our mind to harmonize with our environmental influences—particularly those aspects of the environment resulting from our relationship with other human beings. Although we have free will, our environment determines the nature of our thoughts. Toxic environments produce destructive thought habits, and vice versa. While our innate strengths certainly play a role in our success, our environmental influences can be the reason those strengths flourish or falter.

Both imitation and flattery are gateways to drifting.

The dominating influences to which our mind is most susceptible are those formed by the association with other minds. As the Devil says, "all people absorb and take over, either consciously or unconsciously, the thought habits of those with whom they associate closely." We mimic the thought habits, and then the actions, of others, and this imitation becomes a fixed habit that can be overtaken by the law of hypnotic rhythm.

The process of creating mental and behavioral habits through imitation begins in childhood, when we replicate the thoughts and actions of our parents. The Devil perverts a healthy developmental process by manipulating parents' minds to inadvertently lure their children into drifting. When parents force children to think the same thoughts and believe the same beliefs as them rather than cultivate freedom of thought, they are doing the work of the Devil. In addition, the majority of parents are themselves drifters, so by following their example, their children become drifters as well. When children have their courage and power of independent thought undermined by their parents—and this process continues with teachers, religious educators, and other societal influences, as chapter 18 details—they become prone to the negative workings of hypnotic rhythm early in life.

Find your power supply...and recharge.

Fortunately, we have the power to control our environment. In order to do so, we must stop drifting, take ownership over our thought habits, and choose an environment that fosters positive thinking. The way to do this is through definiteness of purpose, which enables us to cultivate a new mental, spiritual, and physical environment that is conducive to reversing the application of hypnotic rhythm from negative to positive ends.

The most effective environment for fueling your success journey is the one created by a mastermind group. Discussed in detail in chapter 13, a mastermind group is a harmonious alliance of individuals who work together to help each other achieve one another's definite major purpose.

Steps to Self-Determination

What environmental influences are currently negatively impacting your efforts to attain your definite major purpose, either directly or indirectly? Make a plan for transforming your current environment or creating a new one to better support your success journey.

CHAPTER 10

◆

TIME

Time is nature's seasoning influence through which human experience may be ripened into wisdom.

TIME IS SIMPLY ANOTHER way of conceptualizing hypnotic rhythm. Time and hypnotic rhythm are part and parcel of the same natural force that solidifies thought habits, making it increasingly difficult to break them. This force either rewards or penalizes us according to the nature of our thought habits. If our dominating thoughts are negative, then Time will cement the habit of negative thinking. Every additional minute you spend engaging in negative thinking, you are giving Time the opportunity to render the thought habit permanent through the law of hypnotic rhythm. The same rule applies to positive thinking: the more you practice positive thinking, the more likely Time will grant it permanence. The time that is required to fix permanently one's thoughts habits differs for each individual, but it ultimately depends on the object and nature of your thoughts.

> **What do you think about…time healing all wounds?**
> Time cannot heal our hurts or solve our problems without our intentionality and active participation. As the great stream of life that ushers us toward the thought habits we cultivate, Time modifies facts, values, and human relationships according to the principles through which we relate to ourselves, society, and other individuals. But it is always striving for harmony: whatever we sow in terms of negative or positive relationships, we will harvest the same.

Wisdom is the fruit of maturity.

Time not only makes thought habits permanent, but it also ripens human experience into wisdom. This type of knowledge can be cultivated only through the passage of time. It differs from accumulated knowledge because it does not come automatically with the aggregation of information. It does not derive purely from extended study or from mentorship; the knowledge received from these sources must be seasoned with time, positive thinking, and voluntary effort. For this reason, wisdom is not typically obtained until after the age of 40. Prior to that, most people are focused on accumulating knowledge and organizing it into definite plans.

"Wisdom is the ability to relate yourself to nature's laws so as to make them serve you, and the ability to relate yourself to other people so as to gain their harmonious, willing cooperation in helping you to make Life yield whatever you demand of it."

Wisdom comes only to non-drifters with positive dominating thoughts. It cannot be abused by being applied for questionable or evil purposes; it must always be directed toward positive, constructive ends. As such, its aim is usually providing useful service to others.

How can you convert knowledge into wisdom? The formula the Devil provides is "Time plus the desire for wisdom." In order to obtain dependable, time-tested knowledge, we need to understand how to harness the power of hypnotic rhythm to drive our personal growth. This involves searching out the keys to harmonious alliance with natural law and with other people. Adversity and failure are also effective means for shaping knowledge into wisdom—*if* we voluntarily seek out the lessons and opportunities contained in them.

Steps to Self-Determination

What wisdom are you hoping to obtain as you mature? List five subjects, concepts, or ideas about which you would like mature, time-tested, accurate knowledge, and note steps you might take to convert knowledge about these topics into wisdom.

CHAPTER 11

◆

HARMONY

*Nothing transcends harmony and ordered
relation, which is the deathless force of all
law. It is the essence of the Infinite.*

BEHIND THE ENTIRETY OF existence is an inexorable law that
cannot be violated. It commands that the universe seeks to restore order
and balance in all things. This applies both to Nature as a system and
to its individual elements. Even though individual units of energy tend
toward entropy, or disorganization, there is a counterforce working to
establish harmony.

Ralph Waldo Emerson famously theorized this universal law of harmony as the law of compensation. Describing the dualism by which all
of Nature is structured, Emerson explains that "the same dualism under-
lines the nature and condition of man."

"Every excess causes a defect; every defect an excess. Every sweet hath its sour; every evil its good. Every faculty which is a receiver of pleasure has an equal penalty put on its abuse. It is to answer for its moderation with its life. For every grain of wit there is a grain of folly. For every thing you have missed, you have gained something else; and for every thing you gain, you lose something."[1]

Because of the law of compensation, our efforts will always yield a corresponding result, whether that result surfaces immediately or in the distant future. For this reason, it is extremely important that we are thoughtful about every behavior in which we engage, recognizing that there will be short-term and/or long-term consequences. This law also enables us to take comfort in the fact that all adversity must be balanced by prosperity. Whether we are able to enjoy this prosperity, however, depends on the manner in which we respond to adversity. All adversity presents the seeds of opportunity, but we must identify the potential within difficulty in order to reap the available benefits.

Disorganized minds and bodies produce disordered thoughts and plans.

Because our thoughts seek to harmonize with the dominating influences of our environment, regardless of whether we actively facilitate the process or not, it is crucial that we cultivate an environment that helps us

1   Ralph Waldo Emerson, "The Law of Compensation," in *Essays: First Series* (Boston: Phillips, Sampson, and Co., 1856), 87.

establish and maintain a harmonious body and mind. Once we reach adulthood and it is within our power to control our surroundings, we must actively monitor our mental, spiritual, and physical environment to ensure that its dominating influences are positive. When you identify elements that are negative, remove them immediately. For instance, if you discover an influence of failure consciousness acting on your life, try to surround yourself with successful individuals so that your mind can harmonize with the atmosphere of success consciousness. Another scenario: If you recognize that a business associate is injecting doubt into your organization, seek a new alliance so that your mind does not harmonize with your associate's fear and criticism.

> "No human being owes another any degree of duty which robs him of his privilege of building his thought habits in a positive environment."

What happens if the negative influences in your life are family members? An in-depth answer to that question is found in the chapter on relationships, but here is a succinct response: no relationship, even those with blood relatives, is worth maintaining if it causes you to form the habit of drifting.

Your success and happiness are too important to allow yourself to be sucked into the abyss of negative thoughts because of toxic loyalty. Surround yourself with positive, driven, free-thinking individuals, and your thoughts will harmonize in a powerful, productive way. In addition, when you emit positive thoughts, they will harmonize with and attract positive energy from the spiritual plane, thereby enlarging your intelligence and increasing your momentum.

Our bodies are also subject to the law of harmony. While heredity plays a role in the functioning of our internal system, it is not insurmountable except in very extreme cases. When the individual elements of the physical body are out of harmony with each other, it derails our thought habits. Put another way: disorganized bodies create disorganized minds. Below are the three main causes of dysfunction in the bodily system:

- *Overeating*—The Devil admits, "I cause most people to eat too much food and the wrong sort of food. This leads to indigestion and destroys the power of accurate thought. If the public schools and the churches taught children more about proper eating, they would do my cause irreparable damage." Overindulgence in food, especially unhealthy foods, clogs our bodily system, slowing down cognition. More on the importance of healthy eating is found in the lesson on self-discipline.

- *Intemperance*—The habit of drinking too many alcoholic beverages similarly causes disharmony in the body and in the environment and primes us for drifting. The Devil discloses that he encouraged the spread of alcoholism after World War I in an effort to disrupt the growing tendency of young people to think for themselves. Excessive alcohol consumption not only creates disharmony in the organs, especially the liver, but it also disorders the mind, producing incoherent, frenzied, and overemotional thoughts.

- *Smoking*—After the Devil's success with drinking, he enticed the post-World War II youth to adopt another bad habit—that of smoking. Beyond the physical repercussions, cigarette smoking, like intemperance, induces an individual to succumb to drifting, for "cigarettes break down the power of persistence; they destroy the power of endurance; they destroy the ability to concentrate; they deaden and undermine the imaginative faculty, and help in other ways to keep people from using their minds most effectively." It also "invites looseness in other human relationships." Smoking disorders one's body, mind, relationships.

By abstaining from unhealthy habits like overeating, overdrinking, and smoking; by maintaining a balanced diet; by drinking enough water; and by getting enough sleep, we can ensure our body stays in the most harmonious state possible. Sometimes genetics and the environment exert their influence over the body and illness results, but we can all do our part to maintain the body's rhythmic, harmonious functioning through healthy habits.

Steps to Self-Determination

Can you identify disorder in your current mental, emotional, spiritual, and/or physical state? Are there any environmental influences to which you can attribute your dysregulation? How are any of your own unhealthy behaviors creating disharmony? Make a plan for uprooting negative influences and harmful habits and replacing them with healthy habits that are conducive to harmonious cognition and an efficient bodily system.

CHAPTER 12

◆

CAUTION

*Next to the habit of drifting the most dangerous
human trait is the lack of caution.*

DRIFTERS DEMONSTRATE A LACK of caution by acting before
they think. For example:

- Drifters are not selective about their friends.

- Drifters are not thoughtful about their choice of occupation. They accept the first job that offers them a paycheck.

- Drifters are not cautious with their investments and often end up getting cheated.

- Drifters do not practice proper self-care and end up ill.

- Drifters do not protect themselves from the environmental influence of those living in poverty, so their minds are overtaken by poverty consciousness.

- Drifters do not study the reasons that other people fail and thus invite failure into their own life.

- Drifters do not examine the sources of fear and therefore invite fear in all its forms.

- Drifters do not carefully choose a romantic partner or attend to the principles of harmonious marital relationships and end up failing in marriage.

- Drifters lose friends and allies from a lack of caution in how they relate to their associates.

> "The drifter always moves without exercising caution. He acts first and thinks later, if at all."

Non-drifters, on the other hand, always exercise caution, carefully thinking through their plans before they begin implementing them. For example:

- Non-drifters account for the weaknesses of their associates and make plans to compensate for them.

- Non-drifters protect their interests by creating backup plans in case their initial attempts fail.

- Non-drifters follow up on the progress of their missions, never taking their success for granted.

Caution does not mean acting in fear; it is actually the opposite: non-drifters exercise caution because they are confident in their definite major purpose and recognize the importance of practical plans to their ultimate success.

> **What do you think about...overcaution? Can an individual be too cautious?**
>
> Not really—there is no such thing as overcaution. What people term overcaution is really just an expression of fear. True caution is always exercised in confidence.

Because environmental influences significantly impact your susceptibility to drifting, caution needs to be applied particularly in the selection of your associates and how you relate yourself to them. It is in your best interest to associate only with those individuals who contribute some definite mental, spiritual, or economic benefit through the relationship. This is the duty of every individual who desires happiness and success.

Definiteness matters more than ingenuity.

Planning is the physical expression of caution. In order for your purpose and plans to yield success, they must be built on a foundation of definiteness. As the Devil advises, "Take inventory of all whom you call successful, and observe that their success is in exact proportion to their definiteness of plan and purpose." In fact, regardless of the strength of your plans, you will eventually find success if you possess the quality of definiteness. That does not mean that practical plans are not important, for the speed with which you succeed is dependent on the soundness of your plans. You will meet with success faster with a sound plan that is definitely applied than an unsound plan that is definitely applied, but both will eventually lead to success. After all, weak plans may gain strength when applied with definiteness. A sound plan that lacks definiteness, on the other hand, will not yield success. Indefiniteness opens the mind to negative influences that lead to drifting, thereby degrading the plans and their implementation.

> "The best of plans sometimes misfire, but the person who moves with definiteness recognizes the difference between temporary defeat and failure. When plans fail, he substitutes others but he does not change his purpose. Eventually he finds a plan that succeeds."

Even with a definite plan and a definite purpose, however, an individual might encounter temporary defeat. When plans do fail, people with definiteness and stickability will persist through challenges, analyzing them for the seeds of new plans. They will also consult their mastermind group for assistance in learning from their unsound plans and forming new practical plans. As long as an individual possesses definiteness, he or she will eventually experience success.

In addition to being definite, plans must be just to find long-term success. The law of compensation dictates that people reap what they sow. Plans that lack justness or morality may bring temporary success but not enduring success, which requires the support of time. Time, ever a friend of justice and morality, rights all wrongs, ensuring that people who sow plans backed by negative impulses will eventually be penalized with a failed harvest. Do not make the mistake of coveting the temporary gains yielded by immoral, unjust plans; look ahead to observe the negative results on the horizon.

Steps to Self-Determination

In what areas of your life do you need to exercise more caution? How could injecting your plans with more definiteness boost your success in these areas?

CHAPTER 13

◆

THE MASTERMIND

Noteworthy achievements in all walks of life
come through the application of the Master
Mind (harmonious coordination of two or more
minds working toward a definite end).

THERE IS STRENGTH IN numbers. The mastermind principle harnesses the positive workings of hypnotic rhythm in order to materialize this truth. A mastermind alliance is an arrangement made between two or more individuals who agree to coordinate their minds in order to help each other achieve their definite major purpose. It is more than a network—a mastermind group is significantly smaller, formed with extreme intentionality, and characterized by regular meetings. It is the most important professional alliance you will ever have, so you must select its members very carefully—not based on whom you like, but who will most benefit your success journey by complementing (not replicating) your expertise and experience and keeping you focused on your definite major purpose.

By aligning their thoughts and purposes, mastermind members take advantage of Nature's preference for harmony and enlist the universe to bring them economic and psychic advantages.

- *Economic advantages*—Individuals in a mastermind can coordinate their efforts to generate income. Members help each other identify and obtain access to networking opportunities, supplement each other's knowledge, assess the soundness of plans, and combine efforts in other ways so as to increase one another's power and momentum toward translating desire into material riches.

- *Psychic advantages*—When individuals join forces toward a specific end, working in a spirit of complete harmony, they create a third mind: their spiritual energy is so greatly magnified that an affinity is constructed—a force that increases the energy of every member of the group and provides greater access to Infinite Intelligence.

By reaping financial and spiritual advantages, mastermind members achieve success exponentially faster than those trying to do it on their own. Andrew Carnegie touted the mastermind principle as the secret behind his massive success—as did over 500 others of significant business and professional achievements.

What do you think about...an imaginary mastermind?

Invisible Counselors are a mastermind of the mind—a panel of mentors, both alive and dead, with whom you communicate using the sixth sense. Identify which character traits you would like to possess; then determine which individuals, living or dead, most embody that quality. After creating your list of Invisible Counselors, hold regular meetings with them in which you direct group members to hand over the secret to cultivating the character traits you desire. Observe, too, their manner of discourse so that you can imitate their thought habits and actions. Hill's original council included Emerson, Paine, Edison, Darwin, Lincoln, Burbank, Napoleon, Ford, and Carnegie.

Whether activating the economic or psychic advantages, individuals in a mastermind group should use the association to develop and refine practical plans in the following manner:

- Build a mastermind group that will provide all the support you need to create and/or execute your plans.

- Determine what assistance and expertise you can provide in exchange for group members' cooperation and insight.

- Schedule meetings with your mastermind group at least twice per week.

- Ensure that perfect harmony is maintained between group members.

The last point is especially important because cooperation is critical for the mastermind principle to work. As your mastermind alliance works harmoniously toward a definite aim, remember to dedicate enough time and attention to evaluating the soundness of your plans, as their soundness determines the speed with which you accomplish your purpose. Remember, as well, that no person has enough education, experience, natural talent, and imagination to achieve great success without the help of others.

Steps to Self-Determination

Whom will you invite to form a mastermind group with you (if you have not already formed one)? Remember to select individuals whose experience and expertise complement, not replicate, your own; who will not accept failure as final; and who will encourage independence of thought. After you create a list of desired members, make a plan for inviting them to form an alliance and for scheduling your first session. Include below a list of possible talking points for your first meeting.

CHAPTER 14

POWER

*It is not the mere state of mind known as definiteness
which gives one power. But it is the forces, people,
and knowledge which definiteness attracts.*

POWER REFERS TO THE influence and authority that one culti-
vates through definiteness of purpose and plans. As with all forces in
Nature, power has both negative and positive manifestations. It can
raise a leader at the expense of the follower, or it can enrich both parties. These two types of power are called power by force and power
by cooperation.

Power by force is coercive; it uses propaganda and violence, whether
physical or psychological, to secure unwilling or unknowing followers.
Leaders who govern by force subdue people through the habit of drifting.

The Devil takes credit for appointing all dictators, noting that democracy is the enemy of drifting because it encourages independent thought. As individual initiative is destroyed, those ruled by dictators forfeit their agency, creativity, and willpower, further disempowering them. Yet dictators ultimately fail because the law of compensation returns their force with weakness and because their followers operate on a lower plane of thought, inhibiting the success of the entire collective.

True, longstanding power can be gained only through cooperation. Power achieved through consent empowers all individuals—leaders as well as followers—to coordinate with hypnotic rhythm to achieve greater results.

The Devil is in the details.

The Devil's favorite method of acquiring power over individuals is propaganda, which he defines as "any device, plan, or method by which people can be influenced without knowing that they are being influenced, or the source of the influence." The Devil favors propaganda because of its subtlety: people consume propaganda but are not able to distinguish it from their own thoughts, and soon they begin to police themselves according to this propaganda that they mistakenly associate with their own desires and thought impulses. These individuals then fall prey to drifting because they lose all freedom of thought. People give the Devil "the right to think their thoughts while they are living, and the privilege of taking over what is left of them when they die." The Devil is the greatest propagandist of all time—indeed, fear of the Devil itself is nothing more than propaganda.

> **What do you think about...news media?**
> The Devil admits to mixing propaganda with the news of the world, and the effects are palpable: addiction to sensationalized information and mass fear disguised as caution. Non-drifters consume news media sparingly and possess the ability to discern the threat of negative thought impulses that might induce the habit of drifting.

Only drifters are susceptible to the Devil's machinations. The following is the Devil's preferred method of obtaining control over an individual through the use of propaganda:

- Bribery, especially through:
  - Love
  - Sexual desire
  - Covetousness for money
  - The compulsive desire to receive something for nothing (e.g., gambling)
  - Vanity and egotism
  - Desire to master others
  - Desire for intoxicants and narcotics
  - Desire for self-expression through words and deeds
  - Desire to imitate others
  - Desire for perpetuation of life after death
  - Desire to heroize and worship others
  - Desire for physical food

- Intensifying the desire for the individual's greatest weakness and then inducing numerous failures, encouraging them to give up and quit.

- If the individual obtains what they want, the Devil causes them to overindulge in a desire, picking up adjacent follies in the process.

- The Devil wraps what the individual wants in a package of something they don't want.

Bribery provides the Devil access to an individual's mind, and once he gains a foothold, he can begin to manipulate the person's thoughts. If the Devil encounters an obstacle, he turns the individual's natural desires against him or her and makes the desires a gateway to drifting. And the Devil is not alone in his efforts; those individuals already under the Devil's control are enlisted to warp others' thoughts until they become drifters themselves—first through bribery and, if that fails, through fear or the thought of some misfortune. The Devil has both willing and unwilling workers who lure those on the verge of drifting further away from definiteness, trapping them in destructive thought habits that invite the negative workings of hypnotic rhythm.

Emotional intelligence really is the secret sauce to amassing influence.

In order to protect yourself from the Devil's influences as well as those of his legions, seek to gain power through the following means:

- Maintaining definiteness of purpose

- Controlling your emotions
- Mastering fear
- Privileging the love of definiteness over other objects of love
- Demanding what you want from Life and making it pay

Some might worry that if they follow this prescription, they will become hardened. If you share this concern, remember that definiteness is a primary value that supports, rather than diminishes, quality of life and relationships. For instance, those worried about pursuing definiteness above love should recognize that following a definite major purpose will attract people into their life with whom they might form romantic relationships—partnerships that enhance one's success journey.

> "Every principle of good carries with it the seed of an equivalent danger!"

Power, like every natural desire, can be corrupted to turn a leader into a drifter. In order to avoid self-destruction, those who build power through definiteness must reject greed for power and the love of egotistical expression, which lead to the habit of violating the rights of others and cause individuals to fall prey to the negative application of the law of compensation. Definiteness of purpose, then, can be dangerous if it becomes attached to unjust or immoral ends, or if it is used to feed one's ego. Chapter 19 will explain how service must pair with definiteness of purpose.

Steps to Self-Determination

What forms of propaganda are currently manipulating your thoughts? How have they derailed your success journey thus far? Make a plan to gain power by eliminating the influence of propaganda from your life and cultivating definiteness in its place.

CHAPTER 15

◆

FAITH

"Faith" is the beginning of all great achievement.

FAITH IS NOT A momentary feeling, one that can be added to our thoughts at the drop of a hat. It is a state of mind that must be intentionally cultivated by freeing one's mind from all forms of negative thought and emotional conflict and replacing them with definite belief in something. In other words, faith is definiteness of purpose backed by belief in the attainment of the object of that purpose. Faith and fear cannot coexist in the mind: where fear resides, faith cannot function.

Hypnotic rhythm, that great natural law that seeks to restore harmony and rhythm in everything, provides the physical rationale for faith. Once the brain is free of all emotional conflict, it can establish balance and order, making it more receptive to positive energy and constructive insight from universal intelligence. In this state of mind known as faith, our thoughts can more readily harmonize with thought impulses from the spiritual plane, enabling us to more easily locate ways and means of attaining any desired purpose that accords with natural law. Faith also helps us locate our "other self" and communicate with Infinite Intelligence through the sixth sense. Lack of faith, on the other hand, blocks any communication from the spiritual plane.

Prayer is a request spoken as an assurance.

When we pray in a state of faith, our prayers are always answered—they just might not be answered with the material things or circumstances for which we prayed. This typically occurs because we were praying for something that required the suspension of natural law. Another reason our prayer might not receive the response we anticipated is that we released it in a state of mind that was not in complete harmony with natural law; in other words, we prayed from a position of fear or desperation rather than one of faith and assurance.

The first point reminds us that there are no miracles; natural law must always govern the results of prayer. The second point indicates that:

- We must pray in a positive state of mind devoid of any emotional conflict.

- We cannot pray from a position of fear, which brings only negative results.

- We cannot whine and beg God or the universe to assume responsibility for all our problems or to provide us with everything we want in life. God does not respond to weakness. Moreover, laziness prevents us from using our minds to transmute our desires into reality.

- We cannot use flattery in an attempt to propagandize God.
- We cannot inject a prayer with laziness by using readymade prayers and expect results.

The law of compensation dictates that we will reap what we sow: if we pray from a position of fear, laziness, or deceit, then that is what we will harvest. And the more we cultivate these negative thought habits through prayer, the more likely it is that hypnotic rhythm will take over and render the habits permanent. On the other hand, if we pray with definiteness of purpose and confidence in our eventual success, we will mobilize the laws of nature to identify practical plans for translating our desires into reality.

> "The individual answers his own prayers because he controls his own state of mind, making it positive or negative."

How can you pray with more efficacy? Follow this new method of prayer:

- Go to prayer before you experience adversity so that you are not tempted to pray from a position of fear.
- Don't ask for more material goods and greater blessings; ask to be worthy of what you already possess.
- Express gratitude for the blessings that already crown your efforts, particularly your intangible assets.

Not only does Infinite Intelligence respond well to this approach, but you will also discover a storehouse of blessings already in your possession, strengthening your gratitude and contentment. In this state of mind, you can more readily ask for guidance from Infinite Intelligence on how to attain your primary desires in life.

Dogma leads to drifting.

Is religion a succor or an affliction? The Devil reveals that it can be both, depending on how it is used. The world's churches, however, often serve as vehicles for propaganda.

Religious leaders inculcate fear into their followers: fear of death, fear of the afterlife, and fear of the Devil. The Devil goes so far as to say that "religion is mankind's greatest enemy and my greatest ally, because it dopes the brain of human beings with dogmas founded and maintained on fear, ignorance, and superstition." By keeping people's minds focused on their fears, religious leaders spread the very ideas they claim to attack. As the Devil notes, "The best way to advertise an idea is by attacking it." In other words, by spreading fear of the Devil, religious leaders actually attach people permanently to their fears. For "men come to resemble the thoughts that dominate their minds," and as the thought habit of fear solidifies, the law of hypnotic rhythm takes over, forcing individuals into complete submission to their fear.

> **What do you think about...organized religion?**
> The Devil claims that the world's religions are his greatest weapon for luring people into the habit of drifting for three reasons:

1. They teach his content—but in the name of God.
2. They indoctrinate people with fear.
3. They cause people to be preoccupied with unknown and unknowable hypotheses.

If religions are the Devil's tools, is there such a thing as sin? The Devil says yes, anything one does or thinks which causes one to be unhappy is sin. Happiness comes only from harmony, and harmony derives from thinking and acting in accordance with natural law. Because the law of compensation ensures that we reap what we sow, we cannot be truly happy if we are sowing seeds of destruction. Therefore, we are able to possess peace of mind only through thoughts and behaviors that respect ourselves and other individuals. The Devil lists the following as some common forms of sin:

- Overeating, which leads to ill health and misery
- Overindulging in sex, which destroys willpower and leads to the habit of drifting
- Allowing your mind to be dominated by envy, greed, fear, hatred, intolerance, vanity, self-pity, or discouragement, which are states of mind that lead to drifting
- Cheating, lying, and stealing, which are habits that destroy self-respect and subdue your conscience
- Remaining ignorant, which leads to poverty and loss of self-reliance

- Being physically ill, which indicates a neglect of Nature's laws

- Accepting anything from life that you do not want, which reveals a failure to use the mind

The Devil qualifies the second-to-last point, noting that physical illness is generally, not always, a sin. Sometimes illness is the result of an individual's failure to care for the body according to natural laws, but sometimes it is the result of the natural process of aging or environmental circumstances that extend beyond an individual's control (such as a lack of harmony between man and Nature on a mass scale). Whenever people experience any form of mental or physical misery, they should pinpoint the source of sin and work quickly to uproot it before hypnotic rhythm takes over and renders it permanent.

Warring entities or opposing forces?

God and the Devil are two expressions of the same force—they are simply good and bad expressions of it. The Devil controls the forces of hate, fear, vanity, avarice, greed, revenge, superstition, and lust, while God controls all the positive forces in the world, including love, faith, and hope. The Devil and his opposition are likened to the positive and negative charges in an atom. In the Devil's words: "We represent the positive and the negative forces of the entire system of universes, and we are equally balanced one against the other." For this reason, "neither can take over the other because each controls one half of the power which keeps the universe under organized control."

What we might call God—and what the Devil simply calls his "opposition"—controls positive thought. God is universal energy that enables individuals to attain the material equivalent of their desires. By maintaining control over their minds, people can access this Infinite Intelligence and profit from its insight while living; and when they die and give up their physical body, they can become part of it. Because of this, the Devil argues that "the only form of enduring salvation that is worth a green fig to any human being is that which comes from recognition of the power of his own mind."

The Devil is negative energy and controls negative thought. He is not some caricatured demon with a forked tongue and spiky tail; this image is propaganda used by religions to spread fear. The Devil occupies idle minds and the neglected corners of the human brain, sowing the seeds of negative thought so that he can assume full control. It is important to note that the Devil cannot punish anyone except in their own mind, and this occurs primarily through some form of fear. It does not matter whether the fear is connected with something that exists or does not exist—the emotion of fear itself produces thought habits that attract the negative workings of hypnotic rhythm.

> The Devil "cannot punish anyone, except in that person's own mind through some form of fear."

It is the Devil's purpose to trap as many human beings as possible into the negative functioning of hypnotic rhythm so that he can claim their mental power when they die. As you learned in chapter 1, any mind in a state of fear or disorganization at the moment of death loses its intelligence units to the Devil, whereas a harmonious mind will retain its identity after death. One of the Devil's strongest weapons, then, is the fear of death; other commonly used tools are poverty and ill health, which both discourage accurate thinking.

Steps to Self-Determination

Write two prayers below using the formula for effective prayer outlined in this chapter. Increase your faith by practicing these prayers in a positive, grateful, confident state of mind.

◆

CHAPTER 16

Fear

Fear is a self-generating morass.

FEAR IS MENTAL QUICKSAND that consumes anyone who entertains it. Once you open the door to fear, it becomes nearly impossible to extricate yourself from its grip. Fear paralyzes the reasoning faculty, thereby preventing accurate thinking, and it destroys all personal initiative. As this happens, you will find yourself to be increasingly indifferent and irritable, adding other negative thought habits to your foundation of fear. When hypnotic rhythm finally takes over, your sentence will be served: life in the prison of fear.

This occurs on a mass scale as well: fear is contagious, and as more people give power to fear, entire communities become subject to the habit of drifting. The Great Depression, for instance, was the result of large-scale fear generated by World War I. Fear is a generational curse that can be broken with faith.

The Devil plants the seeds of fears in people's minds, and as these seeds germinate and grow through use, he controls the space they occupy. His approach is so subtle that people believe the fears to be of their own creation. The Devil's six favorite tools for gaining control of the human mind are the following:

- *Fear of poverty*—The fear of poverty inspires poverty consciousness, leading to thought habits characterized by indifference, indecision, doubt, worry, and overcautiousness.

- *Fear of criticism*—The fear of criticism destroys one's creative faculties, one's freedom of thought, and one's initiative. It is what prevents great thinkers from arising. Because of this fear, people do not question dominant narratives, allowing religious, political, and other thought leaders to hypnotize them with false doctrine. The fear of criticism is particularly prominent in individuals whose parents were highly critical of them in childhood, causing them to develop an inferiority complex. It leads to thought habits characterized by self-consciousness, meekness, indecision, inferiority, extravagance, lack of initiative, and lack of ambition.

- *Fear of ill health*—The fear of ill health is closely related to the fear of old age and the fear of death: all three come from humans fearing what happens after they die. It often produces the very symptoms it dreads because disease can begin as a negative thought impulse. It leads to thought habits characterized by an addiction to health fads, hypochondria, self-indulgence, and intemperance.

- *Fear of loss of love*—The fear of loss of love arises when people worry about infidelity or abandonment by their romantic partner. It leads to thought habits characterized by jealousy, fault-finding, injudiciousness with money, and adultery.

- *Fear of old age*—The fear of old age results from concern about the afterlife, poverty in old age, and loss of freedom of thought and activity resulting from the aging process. It leads to thought habits characterized by immaturity, nostalgia, inferiority, and a lack of imagination.

- *Fear of death*—The fear of death similarly results from concern about the afterlife. It leads to thoughts characterized by inaction, a fear of poverty, and religious fanaticism.

Out of the six basic fears, the fear of poverty and the fear of death are the most useful to the Devil. These are the most powerful in eradicating freedom of thought and chaining people to his propaganda. To combat the fear of poverty and the fear of death, remember that both riches and your eternal existence are dependent on your ability to control your thoughts. As chapter 1 explains, life is energy, and it is not destroyed at the moment of the body's physical failure. However, whether this energy disperses or retains its association depends on whether you are free of any fear at the moment of death.

> **What do you think about...the fear of criticism?**
> The fear of criticism limits the great thinkers of the world from sharing their truths. It is the Devil's way of suppressing pioneers, hindering innovation, and keeping humankind bound by the shackles of

stagnant thought. The only way to progress as an individual—and as a society—is to give up people-pleasing tendencies, cultivate independence of thought, and exchange truths openly, without fear of criticism or retribution. There is something worse than not being liked, and that is giving space to negative and idle thoughts, both of which lead to the habit of drifting.

When a fear has grown so much that it dominates all of your thoughts, causing you to feel helpless and to struggle when making decisions, a state of mind known as worry emerges. Worrying results in four negative consequences that should be avoided:

- Worrying transmits destructive thought impulses to others.
- Worrying paralyzes the reasoning faculty (the synthetic imagination) and the sixth sense (the creative imagination).
- Worrying enlists hypnotic rhythm to take over and produce the fear's equivalent.
- Worrying produces a negative, unpleasant personality.

Worry destroys self-confidence and reduces your ability to take action on your dreams. The cure for worry is decisiveness and personal initiative—the focus of the next chapter.

"Keep doubt and fear and worry, and all thoughts of limitation, entirely out of your mind."

Steps to Self-Determination

Which of the six basic fears are you nurturing in your mind? Debunk these fears below, identifying what is irrational and/or unproductive about them. Commit to eradicating them from your mind so that you can make full use of the creative and synthetic imagination.

CHAPTER 17

———— ◆ ————

DECISIVENESS AND INITIATIVE

Keep your own counsel...by reaching your own decisions.

INDECISION IS THE WORST of all human ailments. It destroys initiative and independent thought. Weak, aimless thoughts grant the Devil control over a person's mind, where the Devil can plant the seeds of fear. This is a vicious cycle, as growing fear creates more indecision. When hypnotic rhythm takes over, the procrastinator finds himself or herself completely paralyzed by anxiety and confusion, stuck in limbo and unable to find a path forward.

Thankfully, there is a means of preventing indecision from becoming the hallmark of your life. By thinking for yourself, you can protect your present and turbocharge your future. You have to be able to think independently in order to combat society's propaganda and avoid the Devil's traps of bribery, failure, and fear.

> ### What do you think about...procrastination?
>
> According to the Devil, procrastination and drifting are essentially the same thing. He says, "Any habit which causes one to procrastinate—to put off reaching a definite decision—leads to the habit of drifting." When we put off necessary action, we not only build fear, thereby hindering our creative and logical faculties, but we also make space in our brain for the Devil to plant the seeds of destructive thought habits. Think of a time you've hesitated to start on a project—what has been the result? Very likely, you experienced increased anxiety that further dissuaded you from beginning to work on it. That anxiety led to other negative thought habits, like guilt, shame, and apathy. Once these habits are created, they soon become a rhythm that is incredibly difficult to break.

Because fear and indecision contribute reciprocally to one another's growth, you can cure both by taking initiative and applying decisiveness to the fear(s) with which you struggle.

- *The fear of poverty* can be cured by deciding to make do with whatever financial resources you have.

- *The fear of criticism* can be cured by deciding not to care about what others think, say, or do.

- *The fear of ill health* can be cured by deciding to seek and trust medical professionals for care when you experience any symptoms.

- *The fear of loss of love* can be cured by deciding to live a fulfilling, meaningful life with or without a romantic partner.

- *The fear of old age* can be cured by deciding to accept the aging process.

- *The fear of death* can be cured by deciding to accept one's mortality.

The general habit of worrying can be cured by deciding that nothing is worth the price it brings.

Non-drifters think freely and act decisively on their own terms.

Drifters cannot make decisions, and if they manage to do so, they lack the initiative to act on them. If by chance they are able to take action, they will second-guess themselves, act with hesitation, and consider going back on their decision.

The most common area in which people procrastinate is in choosing a definite major purpose. As they coast through life on autopilot, they develop the habit of drifting—accepting whatever life throws their way and never operating with a clear sense of direction. They will fall into the first job offered to them after graduation, marry the first person who shows romantic interest in them, and make a host of other critical decisions without any intentionality.

Environmental influences and imitation are responsible for adopting the habit of procrastination early in life, and society worsens it in adulthood by causing people to trust external sources for the "truth" rather than their natural instinct.

If you find yourself plagued by procrastination, you can break this habit by taking the following steps every time you encounter a decision that needs to be made:

- Quietly research your options.
- Settle on a course of action.
- Commit to the course of action.
- Take action with courage.

Once you make a decision, you should modify your plan only after prolonged consideration and consultation with your mastermind group. After all, successful people have a habit of making decisions promptly but altering those decisions slowly, if at all. And they do not listen to others' opinions—thoughts that are formed quickly and without sufficient evidence. They attend to the counsel of their mastermind group, who always has their definite chief aim and definite plan at the forefront of their minds. But the most important counsel is always that received in one's own mind.

> "Reach decisions promptly and change them, if at all, slowly and with reluctance, and never without a definite reason."

Steps to Self-Determination

In what areas do you tend to procrastinate in life? Why do you think these are trouble areas for you? What fears might be at the root of them? Whose opinions have you been entertaining that have caused you to distrust your intuition? Make a plan to listen only to your own counsel and that of your mastermind group and to use the decision-making strategies in this chapter to cure yourself of worry and fear.

_____

_____

_____

_____

_____

_____

_____

_____

_____

_____

_____

_____

_____

_____

_____

_____

_____

_____

Develop your resolve and initiative by memorizing and reciting the following statement a couple times per day:

"Tell the world what you intend to do, but first show it." —Napoleon Hill, *Think and Grow Rich*

CHAPTER 18

◆

EDUCATION

The entire public school system is so administered that it helps [the Devil's] cause by teaching children almost everything except how to use their own minds and think independently!

ENVIRONMENTAL INFLUENCES HAVE A profound impact on us because our minds knowingly and unknowingly harmonize with the dominant thought habits of those environments. With education, this process is more potent: educators—which can include parents, school-teachers, religious educators, and other mentors—directly transfer their thought habits to students. Children are the most susceptible to these influences because of their tendency toward imitation. The danger is threefold:

- Educators destroy the habit in children of thinking for themselves.

- Educators diminish independent thought by confusing children's minds with unprovable ideas.

- Educators enforce the acquisition of abstract knowledge without showing students what to do with the knowledge after they obtain it.

Most of the time, of course, the damage is unintentional. Educators think they are doing what is best for their students because they are following the pattern of society. The problem is, that pattern is controlled by the Devil and is meant to drag people into the habit of drifting. As the Devil explains, the work of education is done in the name of "civilization," a concept typically credited to the workings of God; however, the Devil is actually responsible for the machinations of civilization. Moreover, when educators—especially religious educators—convey knowledge about unprovable ideas, they accompany these theories with the seeds of fear about hell and death, creating space in the mind for the Devil to grow the fears and take control.

> "The schools and colleges teach practically everything except the principles of individual achievement. They require young men and women to spend from four to eight years delving into academic unreality and acquiring abstract knowledge, but do not teach them what to do with this knowledge after they get it."

The best education one can receive is from the "university of life."

Rather than learning thought habits that inspire drifting from various formal curricula, children and adolescents should learn from experience, otherwise known as the "university of life," where they can acquire practical knowledge of:

- How to develop and use their minds
- How to adopt and use the thoughts of others
- How to examine facts and organize them into definite plans

What do you think about...experiential learning?
More important than any facts or ideas you can acquire in the public school system is the experiential knowledge you can gain from the "university of life." The most valuable knowledge you can possess is a working knowledge of your own mind, which enables you to harness the power of your thoughts and translate your dominating desires into reality. Hill's success principles, paired with an understanding of hypnotic rhythm, will help keep you out of the grip of the Devil.

The Devil acknowledges that the schools and churches do not need to be replaced, but they do need to be reformed so that they will serve people rather than keeping them in ignorance. He discloses 33 changes that should be made to the public school system so that it builds the habit of independent thought instead of the habit of drifting.

- Allow the students to serve as instructors and the instructors to become the students.

- Privilege experiential learning, especially in practical work relevant to everyday life.

- Teach students how to brainstorm and generate ideas so that they can acquire whatever they need in life.

- Teach students how to budget and use time, emphasizing that time is the greatest asset available to all human beings— and the cheapest.

- Teach students the basic motives that influence people, and show them how to use motives to acquire what they need and want in life.

- Teach students the connection between healthy eating habits and sound health, and help them understand how to select and portion food.

- Teach students the true nature and function of the emotion of sex, and explain that it can be redirected into a force for attaining one's definite chief aim.

- Teach students the importance of definiteness in all things, first and foremost with the choice of a definite major purpose in life.

- Teach students the good and bad applications of habit, using illustrations to make the concept more tangible.

- Teach students how hypnotic rhythm renders thought habits permanent, and help them build habits that lead to independent thought.

- Teach students that God and the Devil are simply names for the positive and negative elements of power, and that they can access the good and avoid the evil through the proper understanding and use of their own mind.

- Teach students the difference between temporary defeat and failure, and show them how to search for the seed of opportunity that accompanies every defeat.

- Teach students to express their thoughts courageously and to accept or reject the ideas of others, always reserving the privilege to rely on their own judgment.

- Teach students to reach decisions promptly and to change them slowly, if at all.

- Teach students that the human mind is the receiving station of universal energy and is responsible for interpreting stimuli that produce thought.

- Teach students to privilege harmony of mind, which is attainable only through self-control.

- Teach students the nature and value of self-discipline.

- Teach students the law of increasing returns, which operates when individuals always give more and better service than is expected of them.

- Teach students to live by the Golden Rule, which also means that everything they do for others they should do for themselves.

- Teach students not to form opinions unless they are backed by facts or beliefs that may reasonably be accepted as facts.

- Teach students that cigarettes, liquor, narcotics, and overindulgence in sex destroy willpower and lead to the habit of drifting. Do not forbid them and discourage independent thought; simply explain their connection to drifting.

- Teach students the danger of believing anything simply because their parents, religious instructors, or someone else says it is true.

- Teach students to face facts, however unpleasant, without resorting to excuses or deceit.

- Teach students to activate their sixth sense to obtain new knowledge and to examine carefully all knowledge received this way.

- Teach students how the law of compensation functions on a daily basis, even in the minutiae of life.

- Teach students that war is murder, no matter how it is cast.

- Teach students that the most effective form of prayer is definiteness of purpose backed by definite plans persistently and continuously applied.

- Teach students that the space they occupy in the world is measured by the quality and quantity of the useful service they render the world.

- Teach students that there is no problem that lacks a solution, and that the solution is often found in the circumstance creating the problem.

- Teach students that the only real limitations are those they set up, or allow others to set up, in their own minds, and that people can achieve whatever they conceive and believe!

- Teach students that textbooks and schoolhouses are helpful resources in developing their minds, but the only schoolhouse of real value is the university of life, wherein one learns from experience.

- Teach students that diplomas and degrees are useful only as wall decorations.

- Teach students to always be themselves and, since they cannot please everybody, to focus on pleasing themselves.

With the implementation of these changes, children would become immune to the habit of drifting and adept at harnessing the positive workings of hypnotic rhythm. After the Devil lists the above recommended changes, he adds the following suggestions:

- These changes should be introduced through the private schools first, which will create a demand for them in the public schools.

- Students should be trained in the psychology of harmonious negotiation between people.

- Students should be trained in the principles of individual achievement that help people attain financial independence.

- Classes should be abolished altogether and replaced with a conference system such as businesspeople employ. Students should receive individual instruction in subjects that cannot be properly taught in groups.

- Every school should have an auxiliary group of instructors comprised of businesspeople, scientists, artists, engineers, and journalists, who would share with students a practical working knowledge of their profession.

These recommendations suggest that the best mode of instruction is that focused on cultivating a working knowledge of the practical affairs of life direct from the original source.

> The Devil "cannot stand up under definite knowledge properly organized into definite plans, in the minds of people who think for themselves."

Steps to Self-Determination

No matter where you are in life, it is crucial that you continue learning, especially to gain practical insight about the workings of your mind. What are the gaps in your current knowledge? What is the purpose for which you desire this knowledge? How might you obtain this knowledge from reliable sources (e.g., personal experience and past formal education, your mastermind group or others' experience and education, public libraries, books and audiobooks, podcasts, and special training courses)?

CHAPTER 19

SERVICE

When a man becomes consumed by the desire for material possessions and personal power over his fellow men and forgets that his greatest privilege on the earth plane is that of rendering useful service to others, he is creating a weapon of self-destruction.

ONE OF THE BEST ways to overcome adversity is to look for a way to render useful service to others. There are two main reasons for this. The primary one is that service dispels the spirit of fear. It is impossible for negative and positive thoughts to be active in the mind at the same time, so when an individual is operating in a state of mind of generosity and charity, it prevents fear and doubt from taking over. For this reason, the best way to respond to difficulties causing worry is to "find some other person who has greater difficulties and lose yourself in trying to assist him or her." This experience will increase your purpose, drive, insight, and gratitude, thereby placing you in a more effective position to generate powerful prayer. In fact, you cannot make use of the "other self" unless you are operating in a spirit of generosity and service. For these reasons, service is the best antidote to adversity.

> "You will find happiness only by helping others find it!"

Service is also the measure by which our reward is determined. The Devil reveals that the best means of acquiring material and financial resources is "by rendering the greatest amount of service to the greatest number of people possible, through whatever media that present themselves to you." Any definite major purpose that does not serve others lacks the strength of one whose focus is on bettering others' lives. Through the law of compensation, Nature ensures that our efforts are met with proportionate consequences. Service yields assistance from Nature and brings you in contact with other allies who will strengthen your cause.

> ***What do you think about...going the extra mile?***
> Hill's success philosophy encourages individuals to "go the extra mile"—to render more and better service than is required of them. Most people do exactly what is required of them, or what they are paid to do, and no more. Don't follow the path of mediocrity. Go above and beyond by contributing

more without requesting permission and without explicit instruction to do so. You will find that you will advance professionally with ease and speed, develop immunity to failure, and build self-confidence and personal satisfaction.

Steps to Self-Determination

How does your definite major purpose serve others? Does it serve others directly (by providing a direct benefit) or indirectly (by equipping them to help themselves)? If your definite major purpose does not incorporate service, how can it be enlarged through a spirit of generosity?

How do you go the extra mile in your home life? Your professional life? Your finances? In all three of these domains of living, how could you further cultivate the habit of going the extra mile?

CHAPTER 20

RELATIONSHIPS

*Completeness of mind can be attained only by harmony
of purpose and deed between two or more minds.*

THE KEY SUCCESS SECRETS revealed by the Devil might seem contradictory: one, independence of thought is crucial to avoiding the habit of drifting; and two, we need to be in relationship with others to fully engage the positive power of hypnotic rhythm. These ideas can be reconciled in the notion that our relationships should encourage active, untethered thinking. In fact, the Devil goes so far as to say that complete independence of thought can be achieved only through the harmonious coordination of multiple minds. In part, he is referencing the mastermind principle, but the more profound truth he is highlighting is that hypnotic rhythm itself depends on human relationship.

The essence of the law of hypnotic rhythm is balance and harmony; it literalizes the relationships that we establish with each other. We are kept in proper relationship with each other because of the law of hypnotic rhythm. Moreover, hypnotic rhythm ensures that our professional, social, and familial habits become a part of the fabric of our being. Character is nothing more than the workings of hypnotic rhythm: our relationship to ourselves and to others as expressed through thought habits becomes crystallized as personality because of hypnotic rhythm. The Devil describes the process in the following manner:

"Hypnotic rhythm picks up the dominating motives, aims, purposes, and feelings of the contacting minds and weaves these into some degree of faith or fear, love or hatred.

After the pattern has taken definite shape, as it does with time, it is forced upon the contacting minds and made a part thereof. In this silent way does nature make permanent the dominating factors of every human relationship.

In every human relationship, the evil motives and the evil deeds of the contacting individuals are co-ordinated and consolidated into definite form and subtly woven into that all important human trait known as character.

In the same manner, the motives and the deeds of good are consolidated and forced upon the individual. You see, therefore, it is not only one's deeds

> but also one's very thoughts which determine the nature of all human relationships."

The law of hypnotic rhythm is the reason why "most adversities grow out of improper relationships between people."

What is the proper relationship between people?

How can we enlist the positive workings of hypnotic rhythm through our relationships with others? According to the Devil, "the proper relationship is one that brings to all connected with it, or affected by it, some form of benefit." There must be harmony of mind and purpose and a spirit of service. Such a relationship can be made to "yield riches in their highest form, riches in material, mental and spiritual estates." Because the stakes are so high, the Devil instructs that "one's intimate associates should be chosen with as much care as one chooses the food with which one feeds his body, with the object always of associating with people whose dominating thoughts are positive, friendly, and harmonious." The highest-stake relationships are the ones with our:

- Marriage partner
- Co-workers
- Close friends
- Close acquaintances

Casual acquaintances and strangers have little impact on our thought habits. Proper relationships require proper motives, harmonious minds, and an attention to the needs of all parties. Improper relationships can be corrected only in two ways:

- The person causing the improper relationship changes their thought habits.
- The relationship changes composition, either by adding or removing individuals from it.

Choose your marital partner wisely.

Marital relationships can propel partners to success or drag them into failure quicker than any other sort of relationship, which is why a marriage partner must be selected with great care. The Devil explains that "the relationship of marriage brings people under the influence of spiritual forces of such weight that they become the dominating forces of the mind." However, many people drift into marriage, and the habit of drifting—especially when practiced by both partners—attracts the solidifying function of hypnotic rhythm.

People drift into marriage because they begin their relationship with flattery, an improper use of the emotion of sex, or improper motives, and then they exacerbate their habit of drifting through bickering. As they exchange negative words, think negative thoughts, engage in negative acts, and develop negative motives for dealing with each other, all this negative energy further entangles them in a web of misery and discord. The opposite principle holds true: when marriage partners think, act, and speak with generosity of spirit to each other, they are granted freedom from all forms of unhappiness. Ultimately, because of hypnotic rhythm, a marriage will succeed or fail based on the manner in which the participants relate themselves to one another.

Is divorce ever acceptable? The Devil says yes, "minds which do not harmonize should never be forced to remain together in marriage or any other relationship. Friction and all forms of discord between minds leads inevitably to the habit of drifting, and of course to indefiniteness." The same rule applies to familial relationships. Recall the definition of sin as whatever causes physical, emotional, or spiritual misery. It is a far greater sin to remain in a relationship that is bringing one or more parties down through the habit of drifting than it is to separate and regain control over one's life. Duty is a mistaken notion.

> "The first duty of every human being is to himself! Every person owes himself the duty of finding how to live a full and happy life."

Choose your business associates wisely.

After marriage, your business relationships are the next most critical relationship for enhancing or inhibiting your success and happiness. Not only do we spend a significant amount of time with our co-workers, causing the law of hypnotic rhythm to bring us into harmony with our workplace environmental influences, but our professional success is also dependent on our ability to relate to our associates and to others outside of the business. As the Devil explains, it is more important for professionals to know how to relate to each other and to their clients than it is to possess the specialized knowledge required for their profession.

Business leaders who want to succeed will have a firm understanding of human motivation and what sort of minds harmonize naturally with each other. They will succeed to the extent that they can build a team that will mesh well together and coordinate their efforts efficiently and effectively. Therefore, there is no greater asset to the leader than a firm understanding of the law of hypnotic rhythm. The same applies to individuals looking to advance their career: being intentional about how they relate themselves to their co-workers and others outside the organization so that they engage the positive workings of hypnotic rhythm will do more for them professionally than any talent or task they can complete on their own.

Steps to Self-Determination

Proper relationships require proper motives. What motive is guiding your relationship with your spouse or romantic partner? Your family members? Your friends? Your close acquaintances? Your co-workers? Your clients? Can you identify problems with any of these motives? Are the relationships benefiting all parties involved? Determine what changes, if any, need to be made to your relationships to enlist the positive workings of hypnotic rhythm.

Notes

ABOUT NAPOLEON HILL

Napoleon Hill was born in 1883 in a one-room cabin on the Pound River in Wise County, Virginia. He began his writing career at age 13 as a "mountain reporter" for small-town newspapers and went on to become America's most beloved motivational author. Hill passed away in November 1970 after a long and successful career writing, teaching, and lecturing about the principles of success. Dr. Hill's work stands as a monument to individual achievement and is the cornerstone of modern motivation. His book *Think and Grow Rich* is the all-time bestseller in the field. Hill established the Foundation as a nonprofit educational institution whose mission is to perpetuate his philosophy of leadership, self-motivation, and individual achievement. His books, audio cassettes, videotapes, and other motivational products are made available to you as a service of the Foundation so that you may build your own library of personal achievement materials...and acquire financial wealth and the true riches of life.

THE PURPOSE OF THE NAPOLEON HILL FOUNDATION IS TO...

- *Advance the concept of private enterprise offered under the American System*

- *Teach individuals by formula how they can rise from humble beginnings to positions of leadership in their chosen professions*

- *Assist young men and women to set goals for their own lives and careers*

- *Emphasize the importance of honesty, morality and integrity as the cornerstone of Americanism*

- *Aid in the development of individuals to help them reach their own potential*

- *Overcome the self-imposed limitations of fear, doubt and procrastination*

- *Help people rise from poverty, physical handicaps, and other disadvantages to high positions, wealth and acquisition of the true riches of life*

- *Motivate individuals to motivate themselves to high achievements*

The Napoleon Hill Foundation

www.naphill.org

A not-for-profit educational institution dedicated
to making the world a better place in which to live.

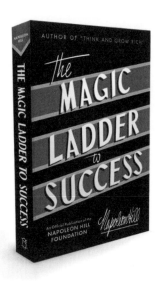 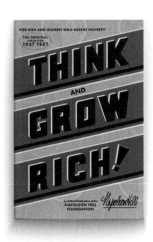 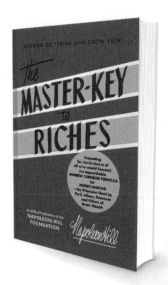